C(
1:
P(

Raintree is an imprint of Capstone Global
Library Limited, a company incorporated in
England and Wales having its registered office
at 264 Banbury Road, Oxford, OX2 7DY –
Registered company number: 6695582

www.raintree.co.uk
myorders@raintree.co.uk

Editorial: Chris Harbo and Gena Chester
Design: Hilary Wacholz
Production: Kris Wilfahrt
Originated by Capstone Global Library Ltd
Printed and bound in India

Superman created by Jerry Siegel and Joe
Shuster. By special arrangement with the
Jerry Siegel family.

ISBN 978 1 4747 6661 6
22 21 20 19 18
10 9 8 7 6 5 4 3 2 1

British Library Cataloguing in Publication Data
A full catalogue record for this book is available
from the British Library

RUFF
RUFF!

BARK
BARK!

SUPER POWERS!

Composite Crisis!

BY ART BALTAZAR AND FRANCO

raintree

a Capstone company — publishers for children

MEANWHILE...

IN THE MIDDLE OF
THE PACIFIC...

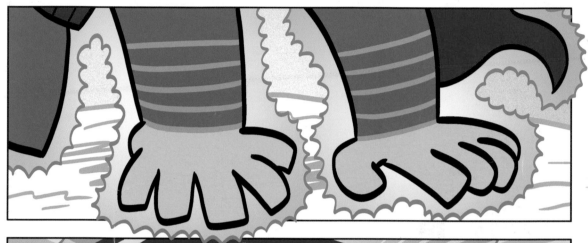

I HAVE TO GET YOU AS FAR AWAY FROM HERE AS POSSIBLE!

YOUR OWN **FORTRESS** IS JUST WHAT YOU NEED!

REST HERE, MY FRIEND.

KEEP AN EYE ON HIM, **KARA**!

WHAT HAPPENED TO HIM?

LET'S JUST SAY YOUR COUSIN **KAL** FLEW TOO CLOSE TO LEX LUTHOR'S KRYPTONITE FORTRESS!

SUDDENLY...

HA!

EXCUSE ME, BUT...

...DID YOU SAY KRYPTONIAN?

YOU WOULDN'T MEAN SUPERMAN, WOULD YA?

GRAB!

HEY! HOW'D YOU DO THAT?

YOU WILL NEVER BE FAST ENOUGH!

HELLO, FLASH.

I KNOW YOUR WEAKNESS.

I WILL FINALLY DEFEAT THE JUSTICE LEAGUE!

NOW, WHERE IS THE KRYPTONIAN?

MEANWHILE ON NEW KRYPTON...

...IN THE CITY OF KANDOR...

OH, JOR-EL, IT'S ALMOST TIME.

REALLY?

WE'D BETTER GO!

GOING SOMEWHERE, JOR-EL?

ZOD!

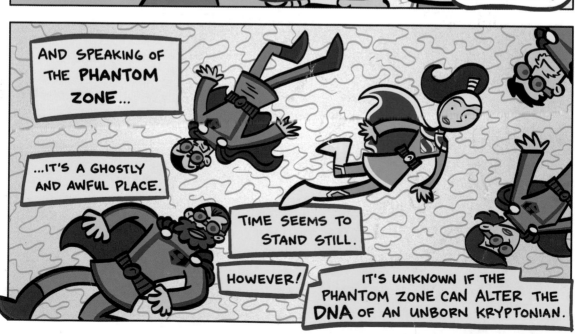

WHAT?

SO, THAT'S WHAT THAT FEELS LIKE.

MEANWHILE...

G'MORNING, KAL!

WOW! WHAT A NAP!

HOW DO YOU FEEL?

TOTALLY ENERGIZED!

THE FORTRESS REALLY WORKS WONDERS!

UH OH!

A DISTURBANCE!

I HEAR IT, TOO!

CENTRAL CITY NEEDS US!

THAT'S FLASH'S CITY, ISN'T IT?

TRUE STORY.

MR. JOR-EL...

YES? HOW IS...?

YOUR WIFE AND BABY BOY ARE FINE.

IT'S A BOY!

YES.

HOWEVER...

...WHEN YOUR WIFE, **LARA**, WAS IN THE PHANTOM ZONE...

...HER AND YOUR SON'S KRYPTONIAN DNA HAVE BEEN ALTERED.

WHAT?

HOW?

WELL, THE PHANTOM ZONE WAS CREATED USING **BRAINIAC** TECHNOLOGY.

SEEMS AS THOUGH THAT SAME TECHNOLOGY INFLUENCED YOUR BABY'S DEVELOPMENT.

WHAT'S WRONG WITH HIM?

NOTHING.

HE'S HEALTHY.

HE HAS GOOD COLOR...

IT'S JUST...

CREATORS

ART BALTAZAR IS A CARTOONIST MACHINE FROM THE HEART OF CHICAGO! HE DEFINES CARTOONS AND COMICS NOT ONLY AS AN ART STYLE, BUT AS A WAY OF LIFE. CURRENTLY, ART IS THE CREATIVE FORCE BEHIND *THE NEW YORK TIMES* BEST-SELLING, EISNER AWARD-WINNING DC COMICS SERIES TINY TITANS, THE CO-WRITER FOR *BILLY BATSON AND THE MAGIC OF SHAZAM!,* AND CO-CREATOR OF SUPERMAN FAMILY ADVENTURES. ART IS LIVING THE DREAM! HE DRAWS COMICS AND NEVER HAS TO LEAVE THE HOUSE. HE LIVES WITH HIS LOVELY WIFE, ROSE, BIG BOY SONNY, LITTLE BOY GORDON AND LITTLE GIRL AUDREY. RIGHT ON!

ART BALTAZAR

FRANCO

FRANCO AURELIANI, BRONX, NEW YORK, BORN WRITER AND ARTIST, HAS BEEN DRAWING COMICS SINCE HE COULD HOLD A CRAYON. CURRENTLY RESIDING IN UPSTATE NEW YORK WITH HIS WIFE, IVETTE, AND SON, NICOLAS, FRANCO SPENDS MOST OF HIS DAYS IN A BATCAVE-LIKE STUDIO WHERE HE HAS PRODUCED DC'S TINY TITANS COMICS. IN 1995, FRANCO FOUNDED BLINDWOLF STUDIOS, AN INDEPENDENT ART STUDIO WHERE HE AND FELLOW CREATORS CAN CREATE CHILDREN'S COMICS. FRANCO IS THE CREATOR, ARTIST, AND WRITER OF *PATRICK THE WOLF BOY.* WHEN HE'S NOT WRITING AND DRAWING, FRANCO ALSO TEACHES HIGH SCHOOL ART.

GLOSSARY

commute long distance to work or school by bus, train or car

composite made up of different parts or elements

delay make someone or something late

disturbance interruption

DNA material in cells that gives people their individual characteristics; DNA stands for deoxyribonucleic acid

energize fill with fuel, or to give energy

general high ranking, important officer in the military

invention new idea or machine

nutrient substance needed by a living thing to stay healthy

pathetic useless or weak

peasant common person

portal large door or path between dimensions, worlds or realms

primitive something in its early stage of development

replenish make full again

VISUAL QUESTIONS AND WRITING PROMPTS

1. BEATING SUPERMAN IS VERY IMPORTANT TO LEX LUTHOR. WHY DO YOU THINK THAT IS?

2. LOOK AT THE DEFINITION FOR "COMPOSITE" IN THE GLOSSARY. WHY DO YOU THINK THE VILLAIN BELOW IS CALLED COMPOSITE SUPERMAN?

3. COMPOSITE SUPERMAN AND UNKNOWN SUPERMAN HAVE FOUGHT EACH OTHER IN THE FUTURE. WRITE ABOUT ONE OF THEIR BATTLES.

4. LOOK AT THE DIFFERENCE IN FACIAL EXPRESSIONS BETWEEN JOR-EL AND LARA. WHAT DOES THIS TELL US ABOUT THEIR OPINIONS ON THEIR NEW BABY?

READ THEM ALL!